FOOD
FOR YOUR
HEALTH

BY HELGA EVANS

Copyright ©1994 Helga Evans
All rights reserved
including the right of reproduction
in whole or in part in any form.

First Edition April, 1994

Published and Distributed by
Helga's Books
3113 Lewis Place
Falls Church, Virginia

Illustrations copyright ©1994 Charlene Rendeiro
Printed in the United States of America

I.S.B.N. 0-9640832-0-5

With a hectic career in the arts and communications (not to mention being "domestically challenged" in the kitchen), Helga has often come to my rescue with menus that please gourmands and the health-conscious alike. She's always had an awareness of healthful but elegant cuisine and I'm delighted that she's finally sharing her knowledge. Brava, Helga!

> — *Renee Chaney*
> *Washington Media Personality*

Our family and guests have savored Helga's gourmet presentations for ten years. We have found them to be beautiful, tasty, and healthful. There always seems to be a scramble for leftovers for days after her dinners.

> — *Lester I. Marion, M.D.*
> *Washington, D.C.*

Helga has been our firm's caterer for a number of years, preparing for us and our clients foods that are not only delicious, but healthy as well.

> — *Norman Oblon, Esq.*
> *Oblon, Spivack, McClelland,*
> *Maier & Newstadt, P.C.*
> *Washington, D.C.*

On many an occasion, Helga's catering has presented our corporation with a sumptuous affair. Her recipes are exciting and the food is superb. I'm sure that her new cookbook, FOOD FOR YOUR HEALTH, will be a great success!

> — *Donald J. Armstrong, M.D.*
> *Philadelphia, PA.*

To My Children:

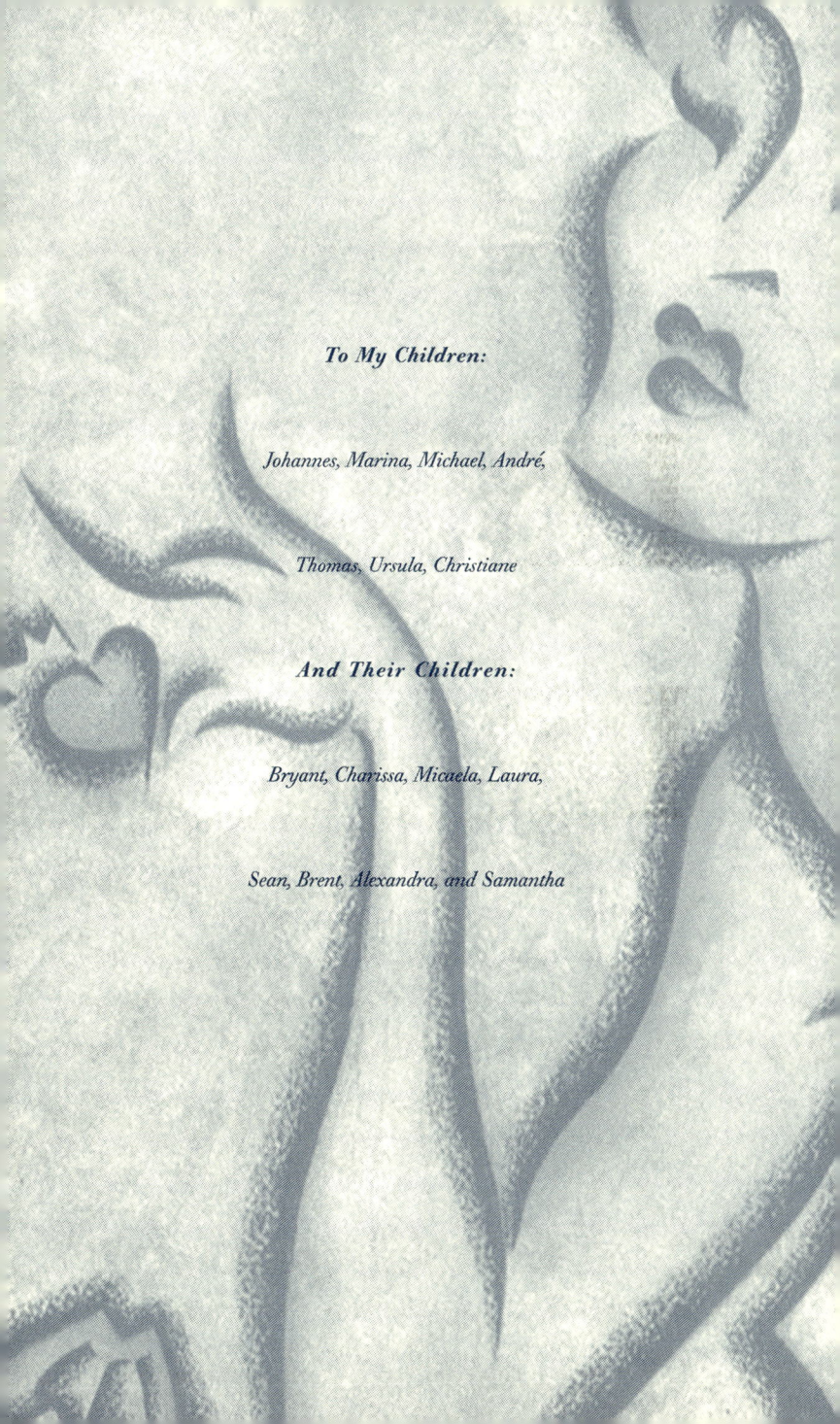

Johannes, Marina, Michael, André,

Thomas, Ursula, Christiane

And Their Children:

Bryant, Charissa, Micaela, Laura,

Sean, Brent, Alexandra, and Samantha

Acknowledgements

*I would like to express my sincere gratitude
to the many people and organizations
who have made this book possible:*

*My sons Michael and Tom, Tom's wife Sesha,
my daughter Chrissy, and our wonderful staff,
for their many years of moral support
and relentless hard work.*

*Our friends at the American College of Cardiology
in Bethesda, Maryland, where we have had
the privilege of providing heart-healthy
food services for the past five years.
To please physicians' tastes who travel here
from all parts of the world is an exciting challenge.
We thrive on their professional critiques.*

*Special thanks go to Bonnie Robeson, for her patience,
nutritional analyses, and suggestions on the recipes
in this book and many others.*

*And last, but not least, I would like to thank
Charlene Rendeiro for her creative cover design
and layout of* FOOD FOR YOUR HEALTH.

Introduction

My love of cooking and entertaining dates back to when our seven children were small. The constant flow of the kids and their friends through the kitchen and dining room made me feel like I was feeding a small army. My husband's career required that we entertain frequently, and, much to my delight, this brought another army of visitors to the house.

By 1980, the children were growing up and I found myself looking for a new and exciting challenge. A catering business seemed the obvious choice! With my son Michael, I founded Helga's Personalized Catering, Inc., in the Washington, DC, area. I'm thrilled that for the past thirteen years we've been developing healthy and delicious menus for an ever-expanding, diverse, and faithful clientele. Our regular clients range from the more than 2000 cardiologists at the American College of Cardiology in Bethesda, MD (all our recipes are heart-healthy and have been approved by the College's nutritional consultant), to a group of 50 senior citizens, to whom we serve healthy dinners every Monday through Friday.

Although semi-retired in 1991, I still make sure to keep actively involved in Helga's by designing strictly personalized menus for our clients. I'm quite excited to pursue a new career... Author. FOOD FOR YOUR HEALTH is a preview of my forthcoming cook book inspired by years of experience in serving healthy menu selections to thousands of appreciative customers. My goal is to share this experience so that you may benefit by watching how and what you, your family, and your guests eat. I hope this booklet will serve as testimony to the fact that you don't need to sacrifice exciting food varieties to stay healthy.

Keep yours eyes open for the expanded version of FOOD FOR YOUR HEALTH!

TABLE OF CONTENTS

ACKNOWLEDGEMENTS *iv*
INTRODUCTION *v*

SOUPS

Wild Mushroom Soup 4
Chunky Turkey Chili 6
Tuscan Minestrone 8
Summer Carrot Ginger Soup 10
Chicken Asparagus Soup 12

APPETIZERS

Smoked Salmon Caviar Roll 16
Mussel Salad Koichi 18
Caponata with Toast Points 20
Crabmeat Charissa Spread 22
Polenta Triangles 24
Escargot in Mushroom Caps 26

SALADS

Couscous Salad with Tropical Fruit 30
Sesha's Potato String Bean Salad Provençale 32
Salmon Orzo Salad 34
Sami's Summer Corn Salad 36
Duck Salad Micaela 38

Entrees

Chicken Dijon 42

Shrimp Carambola Bryant 44

Polish Stir Fry with Turkey Sausage 46

Basque Turkey Casserole 48

Seafood Pasta Pierre 50

Elegant Tuna Patties with Caviar Sauce 52

Don's Citrus Broiled Cornish Hens 54

Quail Alexandra 56

Grilled Salmon Marina 58

Angel Hair Pasta with Escargot 60

Pork Tenderloin Brent 62

Pasta Primavera Light 64

Chicken Roma 66

Jamaican Chicken Breast 68

Desserts

Omi's Crushed Pineapple Pie 72

Sean's Floating Island 74

Raspberry Fool 76

Baked Apple in a Jacket 78

Laura's Strawberry Delight 80

Mail Order Forms 83

Food for your Health

Wild Mushroom Soup

§

Chunky Turkey Chili

§

Tuscan Minestrone

§

Summer Carrot Ginger Soup

§

Chicken Asparagus Soup

Soups

WILD MUSHROOM SOUP

1 1/2 lbs.	Shiitake mushrooms, cleaned and cut into strips with stems cut off
1	Medium onion, minced
1/4 cup	Puritan oil
•	Low sodium salt and pepper to taste
6–7 cups	Low sodium chicken broth
1/2 cup	Chopped parsley
1/2 cup	Sherry
3/4 cup	All purpose flour

Sauté onions in oil until golden brown. Add mushrooms, salt and pepper, and sauté for a few mintues. Add flour and keep stirring until it becomes a walnut color. Remove from heat and stir in cold chicken broth to avoid lumps. Return to the heat and bring to a boil and simmer for about 15 minutes. Add sherry, parsley and serve.

Yields: 10 Servings

Cal.: 123   *Sod.:* 8 mg   *Fat:* 7.2 g   *Chol.:* 0 mg

Calorie, sodium, fat, and cholesterol counts stated are per serving for each recipe.

Notes

§

CHUNKY TURKEY CHILI

1	Small onion
2	Garlic cloves
3	Stalks celery, quartered
1	Green bell pepper, quartered
2 tsp.	Puritan oil
2	Carrots, quartered
8 oz.	Uncooked, diced turkey breast
1 cup	Dry red wine
1–2 tbsp.	Chili powder
1 tbsp.	Fresh chopped thyme, **or** 1 tsp. dried
1 tbsp.	Fresh chopped oregano, **or** 1 tsp. dried
1 tsp.	Spicy salt-free vegetable seasoning
28 oz.	Crushed Italian plum tomatoes, in puree
15 oz.	Kidney beans, drained and rinsed
15 oz.	Chick peas, drained and rinsed

Coarsely chop the onion, garlic, celery, carrots, and green pepper in a food processor or blender; then saute for three minutes in the oil, in a non-stick 2-quart sauce pan. Add the diced turkey and sauté for five minutes, stirring constantly. Add the remaining ingredients, stir, and bring to a simmer. Taste and adjust the seasonings. Cover and simmer for one hour, stirring occassionally to prevent sticking.

Yields: 8 1¼ cup Servings

Cal.: 231   *Sod.:* 506 mg   *Fat:* 3 g   *Chol.:* 25 mg

Notes

§

TUSCAN MINESTRONE

1 cup	Dry kidney beans
1 tbsp.	Extra-virgin olive oil
3	Cloves garlic, minced
1 cup	Canned cannellini or garbanzo beans, drained and rinsed
1/2 tsp.	Crushed red pepper flakes
1	Leek (white part only), sliced and washed
1/2 cup	Orzo
2 1/2 qts.	Water or low sodium chicken broth
3	Large carrots, sliced
3	Stalks celery with leaves, sliced
1 cup	Sliced fresh green beans, chopped
1 1/2 cups	Salt-free tomato sauce
1	Bay leaf
1/2 cup	Red wine
1 tbsp.	Basil and Oregano
2	Zucchini, coarsely chopped
1	Onion, coarsely chopped
1 14.5 oz.	Can sodium-reduced stewed tomatoes, **or** peeled, chopped tomatoes
1 10-oz.	Package frozen spinach, defrosted and drained, **or** 2 cups washed and shredded fresh spinach
•	Low sodium salt to taste

Cover the beans with water and soak overnight. Place the oil in a 6-quart saucepan, add the drained beans, garlic, bay leaf, red pepper flakes, and onion; sauté for five minutes. Add the water or broth, bring to a boil, add red wine, simmer for one hour. Add the leek, carrots, green beans, tomato sauce, basil and oregano, low sodium salt and pepper and cook for 30 minutes. Add the zucchini, remaining beans, and tomatoes and cook 15 minutes. Add the orzo and spinach and cook for 15 minutes.

Yields: 8 Servings

Cal.: 130 *Sod.: 133 mg* *Fat: 1.5 g* *Chol.: 0 mg*

Notes

§

. . . .

. . . .

SUMMER CARROT GINGER SOUP

5	Large carrots, peeled and sliced
3	Slices of fresh ginger (size of one quarter), minced
½	Medium onion, minced
6 cups	Canned low-sodium chicken broth (If vegetarian, use water)
•	Low sodium salt and pepper to taste
½ cup	Orange juice
1 tsp.	Orange zest, minced
½–1 cup	1% Fat milk
3 tbsp.	Puritan Oil
1½ tbsp.	Sugar
•	Black sesame seeds for garnish (optional)

Sauté onions and ginger in oil. Stir in sliced carrots and cook for about five minutes. Add salt, pepper, orange juice and zest, sugar, chicken broth **or** water. Bring to boil, lower heat and cook for 35–45 minutes. Strain off liquid and reserve. Puree vegetables and add back to reserved liquid and chill. Before serving, carefully add milk adjusting to desired consistency, sprinkle with sesame seeds and serve.

Yields: 8 Servings

Cal.: *125*   ***Sod.:*** *80 mg*   ***Fat:*** *8 g*   ***Chol.:*** *1.25 mg*

Black sesame seeds may be purchased at your local oriental market.

Notes

§

Chicken Asparagus Soup

1	Medium onion, chopped
1 tbsp.	Fresh garlic, minced
1	Stalk celery, chopped
1 lb.	Chicken breast without skin, and trimmed of all fat
1 lb.	Fresh asparagus, chopped on the bias into 1/2" pieces
•	Low sodium salt and pepper to taste
2 cups	Cooked rice or small pasta
6 cups	Water
•	Vegetable spray

Sauté onions, celery, and garlic in vegetable spray. Top with chicken, add water, salt and pepper; bring to a boil. Simmer on low for 1/2 hour. Add asparagus and simmer for another 20 minutes. Add 1 1/2–2 cups of cooked rice or small pasta.

Yields: 8 Servings

Cal.: 210   *Sod.:* 80 mg   *Fat:* 2 g   *Chol.:* 45 mg

Notes

§

SMOKED SALMON CAVIAR ROLL

§

MUSSEL SALAD KOICHI

§

CAPONATA WITH TOAST POINTS

§

CRABMEAT CHARISSA SPREAD

§

POLENTA TRIANGLES

§

ESCARGOT IN MUSHROOM CAPS

APPETIZERS

SMOKED SALMON CAVIAR ROLL

1/4 cup	Non-fat sour cream
1 tbsp.	Red Romanoff Caviar
•	Sprinkle lemon-herb seasoning
1/8 tsp.	Fresh chopped dill, reserve remaining dill sprigs for garnish
1 tbsp.	Minced spring onions
3 oz.	Smoked salmon, pre-sliced

Blend all ingredients, except salmon and caviar, in a bowl until smooth. Gently fold in caviar and chill for a few hours.

Spread mixture onto salmon slices and roll up. Chill again.

One hour before serving, slice into thin slices. Serve on top of cucumber slices or crackers and garnish with a fresh sprig of dill.

Yields: 18 Pieces

Cal.: 16   *Sod.:* 35 mg   *Fat:* 1 g   *Chol.:* 10 mg

Notes

§

MUSSEL SALAD KOICHI

Steam Mussels:

2 1/2 dz.	Mussels
4 tsp.	Olive oil
2 tsp.	Fresh garlic, minced
1 1/2 cups	Dry white wine
•	Pinch of red pepper flakes

Wash mussels in cold water two times. Remove beards; scrub shells to remove sediment. Heat oil in skillet over medium heat; sauté garlic until soft, but don't brown. Add mussels, wine, and red pepper flakes, cover and steam until mussels open. Remove pot from heat and discard any unopened mussels. Remove mussels from shell. Reserve shells.

Marinade:

1/2 cup	Olive oil
1/4 cup	White vinegar
1/4 cup	Light soy sauce
1 tbsp.	Minced ginger
1 tbsp.	Minced garlic
•	Red pepper flakes to taste
2–3 tbsp.	Minced fresh cilantro
14–16	Shiitake mushrooms, stems removed and finely chopped, sautéed in 2 tbsp. oil, and cooled (for dried shiitake, pre-soak in water for 30 minutes)

Mix all ingredients in mixing bowl except mushrooms. Gently toss mushrooms and mussels in marinade and marinate for one hour. Refill shells with mussels and mushrooms to serve.

Yields: 6 Servings

***Cal.:** 230*   ***Sod.:** 350 mg*   ***Fat:** 18 g*   ***Chol.:** 15 mg*

NOTES

§

....
....
....
....
....
....
....

Caponata with Toast Points

1	Red pepper, cut into small cubes
1	Green pepper, cut into small cubes
1 lb.	Eggplant, diced with skin on
•	Low sodium salt and pepper to taste
1/3 cup	Olive oil
3 stalks	Celery, sliced
2	Carrots, sliced and cut in half
1 lg.	Onion, minced
1 tbsp.	Minced garlic (optional)
1 16-oz. can	Low sodium tomato paste
1 tbsp.	Sugar
1/2–3/4 cup	Red wine vinegar
4 tbsp.	Capers
1/2 cup	Minced pitted black olives
1/2 cup	Minced fresh parsley
1 head	Red leaf lettuce for garnish

Sprinkle eggplant with salt and leave for one hour, to draw out bitter juices. Squeeze all water out with paper towel. Heat oil in a pan, add onions and garlic, sauté for a few minutes until golden, add celery, carrots, and peppers, keep stir frying.

After three minutes, add eggplant and sauté with spices until limp. Add all other ingredients, cover and simmer until flavors are completely blended, about twenty minutes. Vegetables should be a little crunchy.

Serve on a bed of lettuce with toast points or crackers.

Yields: 8 Servings

***Cal.:** 120*   ***Sod.:** 298 mg*   ***Fat:** 6.8 g*   ***Chol.:** 0 mg*

NOTES

§

....
....
....
....
....
....
....
....
....

CRABMEAT CHARISSA SPREAD

1 16-oz. can	Artichoke hearts, drained
1/2 cup	Cholesterol-free mayonnaise
1/4 cup	Grated parmesan
1/4 cup	Minced spring onions (optional)
•	Low sodium salt and pepper to taste
1/8 tsp.	Cayenne pepper
1 tbsp.	Lemon juice
1 cup	Fresh lumpfish crabmeat (pick through for shells)

Add all ingredients except crabmeat in a food processor. Pulse until finely chopped. Remove, and mix in crabmeat. Bake in preheated 350 degree oven, until golden brown for about 30 minutes.

Serve with crackers. Can be served room temperature, if preferred.

Yields: 12 Servings

Cal.: 107   *Sod.:* 355 mg   *Fat:* 7 g   *Chol.:* 7 mg

Notes

§

POLENTA TRIANGLES

5 cups	*Water*
1 tsp.	*Low sodium salt*
1 ½ cups	*Polenta corn meal*
2	*Slices Monterey jack cheese*
•	*Tobasco to taste*

In large saucepan, bring water to a boil. Add salt. Add polenta very slowly, stirring continously with a wooden spoon. Reduce heat to low, add tobasco to taste, and simmer, stirring, until polenta is thick and smooth. Pour into lightly greased 8" square pan. Let cool until firm. Cut polenta (20) into triangles and top each with a smaller triangle of cheese. Just before serving, heat polenta triangles for a few minutes in a preheated 300 degree oven, or in a skillet over low heat until cheese softens.

Yields: 8 Servings

Cal.: *100*   ***Sod.:*** *50 mg*   ***Fat:*** *2.5 g*   ***Chol.:*** *5 mg*

Notes

§

ESCARGOT IN MUSHROOM CAPS

12	*Hand-picked, medium-size mushrooms, cleaned and stem removed*
1 tbsp.	*Crushed fresh garlic*
1 tbsp.	*Olive oil*
1 tbsp.	*Diet margarine*
1 can	*Escargot (snails), 12–14 count, drained and washed thoroughly*
2 tbsp.	*White wine*
•	*Low sodium salt and pepper to taste*
¼ cup	*Chopped parsley for garnish*

Sauté garlic in oil and margarine on medium heat, until golden brown. Add snails and mushroom caps, upside down. Sprinkle with salt and pepper. Turn mushrooms over, add wine and cover. Cook for a few minutes. Remove mushroom caps to plate, fill with snails. Reduce sauce and spoon over mushrooms. Sprinkle with parsley.

Yields: 4 Servings (12 mushrooms)

Cal.: 125   *Sod.: 100 mg*   *Fat: 6 g*   *Chol.: 50 mg*

Notes

§

Couscous Salad with Tropical Fruit

§

Sesha's Potato String Bean Salad Provençale

§

Salmon Orzo Salad

§

Sami's Summer Corn Salad

§

Duck Salad Micaela

SALADS

Couscous Salad with Tropical Fruit

1 pkg.	*Couscous, cooked according to instructions on box, and cooled*
3	*Lemons, squeezed*
½ cup	*Olive oil*
2 tbsp.	*Balsamic vinegar*
¼ tsp.	*Lemon pepper*
1 tsp.	*Allspice*
⅓ tsp.	*Coriander (ground)*
1 tbsp.	*Mint, chopped*
1	*Mango, peeled and diced into little cubes*
1	*Papaya, peeled, seeded, and diced into little cubes*
1	*Bunch spring onions, chopped*
3	*Slices ginger (size of a dime), finely chopped*
•	*Sprinkle curry (optional)*
1	*Ripe pear with peel, cored and diced*
1	*Red pepper, diced*
•	*Low sodium salt and pepper to taste*

Combine all ingredients in mixing bowl and toss gently. Chill and serve.

Yields: 6-8 Servings

Cal.: *246*   **Sod.:** *30 mg*   **Fat:** *17 g*   **Chol.:** *0 mg*

Notes

§

SESHA'S POTATO STRING BEAN SALAD PROVENÇALE

| 10 | Medium red bliss potatoes, cut into quarters, added to boiling salt water |
| 1 ½ lbs. | Fresh, cleaned, string beans, blanched in salt water, drained and rinsed under cold water to keep crisp. |

Dressing:

½ cup	Dijon mustard
1 tbsp.	Minced garlic
2 tbsp.	Minced onions
¾ cup	Olive oil
½ cup	Red wine vinegar
1 tbsp.	Fresh chopped oregano
1 tbsp.	Fresh chopped rosemary
1 tsp.	Red pepper flakes
1	Thinly sliced red onion for garnish
•	Pinch of low sodium salt

Boil potatoes until tender. Rinse and cool. Combine with cooked string beans. In mixing bowl, mix dressing together. Add dressing to potatoes and string beans, and gently toss by hand, so as not crush potatoes and beans. Garnish with red onion rings.

Yields: 8 Servings

Cal.: 212   ***Sod.:*** 193 mg   ***Fat:*** 3 g   ***Chol.:*** 0 mg

Notes

§

SALMON ORZO SALAD

1 1/2 cups	Dry Orzo pasta, cooked al dente
4	Spring onions, diced
1/2 cup	Minced parsley for garnish
3	Italian plum tomatoes, diced
1 tbsp.	Capers, drained
1 lb.	Poached salmon, broken up
•	Low sodium salt to taste
•	Lemon pepper to taste
1/4 lb.	Fresh spinach, cleaned, rolled and sliced into strips

Dressing:

1/4 cup	Olive oil
1/4 cup	Garlic red wine vinegar
2	Fresh lemons, squeezed
3/4 tsp.	Low sodium salt
•	Freshly ground pepper to taste
1 tsp.	Oregano
1 tsp.	Basil

Drain orzo thoroughly and immediately transfer to a large bowl. Toss orzo with vinaigrette while still hot and add the rest of the ingredients except for parsley, tossing gently. Sprinkle with parsley just before serving. Serve room temperature.

Yields: 6 Servings

***Cal.:** 320*   ***Sod.:** 240 mg*   ***Fat:** 15 g*   ***Chol.:** 170 mg*

Notes

§

....
....
....
....
....
....

Sami's Summer Corn Salad

1	Head red leaf lettuce, washed and broken into bite size pieces
1	Head romaine lettuce, washed and broken into bite size pieces
2	Ripe, homegrown tomatoes, cut into 3/4" cubes
3	Ears, cooked white corn, removed from cob
1	Cucumber, peeled and cut into 3/4" cubes
1	Vidalia onion, thinly sliced
2 stalks	Broccoli flowerets
2 12-oz. cans	Tuna, packed in water
1 cup	Croutons

Dressing:

1	Diced kosher dill pickle
1/2 cup	Low fat mayonnaise
1 tbsp.	Ketchup
1/4 cup	Oil
2 tbsp.	Vinegar
•	Low sodium salt and pepper to taste

Mix dressing ingredients together with a whisk.

Mix lettuce together, toss with some dressing, and place on serving platter. Compose your own creative design of vegetables and tuna on top of lettuce bed, and top with croutons. Offer remaining dressing at side. This is a good summertime recipe and a great way to use up leftover corn on the cob!

Yields: 8 Servings

Cal.: 241   *Sod.: 520 mg*   *Fat: 14 g*   *Chol.: 39 mg*

Notes

§

....

....

....

....

....

....

DUCK SALAD MICAELA

2	Boneless duck breast
1/4 cup	Broken walnut pieces
1 tbsp.	Fresh chopped parsley
2 tsp.	Minced fresh chives
1 head	Boston bibb lettuce, washed and broken into bite-size pieces
2	Naval oranges, peeled and sectioned

Dressing:

3 tbsp.	Sherry vinegar or red wine vinegar
1 tsp.	Dijon style mustard
1/4 tsp.	Low sodium salt
1/8 tsp.	Freshly ground pepper
1/2 cup	Walnut oil

Preheat broiler. Broil duck breast skin side up, until skin is crispy and brown. Remove skin, cool and slice breasts into thin diagonal slices (approx. 1/8").

In bowl whisk vinegar, mustard, salt substitute, and pepper until blended. Gradually whisk in walnut oil. Place duck in shallow dish. Spoon half the dressing over and sprinkle with parsley and chives. Marinate at room temperature for 30 minutes. Toss the lettuce with the remaining dressing. Place lettuce on plates, arrange duck slices and orange sections on top like a flower pattern. Sprinkle with walnut pieces. Serve at room temperature.

Yields: 4 Servings

Cal.: 567   *Sod.:* 121 mg   *Fat:* 50 g   *Chol.:* 35 mg

NOTES

§

....
....
....
....
....
....
....
....
....

Chicken Dijon

§

Shrimp Carambola Bryant

§

Polish Stir Fry with Turkey Sausage

§

Basque Turkey Casserole

§

Seafood Pasta Pierre

§

Elegant Tuna Patties with Caviar Sauce

§

Don's Citrus Broiled Cornish Hens

§

Quail Alexandra

§

Grilled Salmon Marina

§

Angel Hair Pasta with Escargot

§

Pork Tenderloin Brent

§

Pasta Primavera Light

§

Chicken Roma

§

Jamaican Chicken Breast

Entrees

CHICKEN DIJON

| 2 lbs. | Boneless chicken breast, skin removed and trimmed of all fat |

Dressing:

1 ½ cups	Puritan oil
2 cups	Honey
1 ½ cups	Dijon mustard
6 tbsp.	White vinegar
1 ½ tsp.	Lemon juice
¾ tsp.	Red pepper flakes
¾ tsp.	Granulated garlic
•	Low sodium salt to taste

Mix all ingredients in mixing bowl. Pour over chicken and marinate for one hour. Broil 10–15 minutes, or until done.

Yields: 8 Servings

Cal.: *300*   ***Sod.:*** *205 mg*   ***Fat:*** *10 g*   ***Chol.:*** *100 mg*

Notes

§

SHRIMP CARAMBOLA BRYANT

3–4 tbsp.	Low fat margarine
1 1/2 lbs.	Medium shrimp, peeled and deveined
4	Small Carambolas (star fruit), sliced thin, cross-wise
2 tbsp.	Minced fresh cilantro
2 tbsp.	Fresh lemon juice
1 1/2 tsp.	Sugar
1/4 tsp.	Anise seeds (optional)
4	Spring onions, minced
1/8 tsp.	Red pepper flakes
•	Low sodium salt and pepper to taste

Heat margarine in large skillet. Add shrimp and star fruit, and sauté for a few minutes. Add all other ingredients, cook for five minutes. Adjust seasonings. Serve over rice.

Yields: 8 Servings

Cal.: 144   *Sod.:* 70 mg   *Fat:* 4 g   *Chol.:* 130 mg

Notes

§

POLISH STIR FRY WITH TURKEY SAUSAGE

12 oz.	Bow tie pasta, boiled al dente
1 lb.	Grated cabbage (cole slaw mix)
1 1/2 lbs.	Polish turkey sausage, peeled and sliced
•	Low sodium salt and pepper to taste
•	Red pepper flakes for bite
2 tbsp.	Olive oil
1	Medium onion, chopped
1/4 cup	White vinegar
•	Pinch of sugar
1 tbsp.	Sweet paprika
1 tsp.	Minced, fresh garlic

Sauté onions and garlic in hot oil for a few minutes, until golden. Add sausage and cabbage, and stir fry until cabbage is wilted. Add pasta, vinegar and all spices. Heat thoroughly and serve.

Yields: 6 servings

Cal.: 525   *Sod.:* 316 mg   *Fat:* 38 g   *Chol.:* 27 mg

Notes

§

BASQUE TURKEY CASSEROLE

2 lbs.	Ground turkey
½ cup	Minced onions
1 tbsp.	Minced garlic
½ cup	Puritan oil
1 lb.	Rotini pasta
1 tbsp.	Rosemary
1 tsp.	Sage
1 medium	Green pepper, cubed
1 medium	Yellow pepper, cubed
1 medium	Green zucchini, cubed
1 tbsp.	Garlic, minced
4 cans	Condensed tomato soup
8 oz.	Light cream cheese
•	Low sodium salt and pepper to taste

Bring pot of water to boil. Add salt and rotini pasta. Cook about 10 minutes (undercook a little bit), drain off hot water, and rinse pasta with cold water. Brown the first four ingredients in a skillet, drain off fat, add vegetables, herbs, more garlic, salt, pepper and cook for another 5-10 minutes. Blend the cream cheese with a mixer until soft and mix in with the meat and vegetables. Add tomato soup and rotini pasta. Adjust salt and pepper to taste. Bake in pre-heated 400 degree oven for 30-35 minutes and serve.

Yields: 8-10 Servings

Cal.: 653   *Sod.:* 226 mg   *Fat:* 30 g   *Chol.:* 100 mg

Notes

§

SEAFOOD PASTA PIERRE

12	Fresh Italian plum tomatoes, cut into small cubes
2 tbsp.	Minced garlic
1	Medium onion, minced
2 tbsp.	Olive oil
1	Bottle clam juice
1 1/2	Pints light cream
1 cup	White wine or dry Vermouth
1/4 cup	Vodka
1 tsp.	Pepper flakes
1 tbsp.	Thyme
1 tbsp.	Oregano
2 tbsp.	Fresh basil, cut into strips (extra leaf for garnish)
1/8 tsp.	Saffron
1 lb.	Spaghetti, cooked al dente and drained
1 1/2 lbs.	Cleaned string beans boiled for five minutes, then cooled
1 lb.	Medium shrimp, cleaned

Sauté onion in olive oil until translucent, add tomatoes and garlic with all spices. Cook for five minutes, add clam juice, cream, and wine, bring to a full boil. Cook for fifteen minutes uncovered, to thicken.

Add cooked pasta and beans, mix well, add shrimp and vodka, cook on medium heat, covered, until shrimp are pink. Taste and adjust spices. Garnish with fresh basil leaf.

Yields: 6–8 Servings

Cal.: *745*   ***Sod.:*** *43 mg*   ***Fat:*** *22 g*   ***Chol.:*** *240 mg*

Shrimp are high in cholesterol, but an occasional treat is absolutely acceptable in modest portion.

NOTES

§

....
....
....
....
....
....
....
....

ELEGANT TUNA PATTIES WITH CAVIAR SAUCE

3 12½-oz. cans	Tuna packed in water, drained
1	Small onion, diced
1	Stalk celery, finely diced
1 cup	Low fat mayonnaise
1 tsp.	Prepared mustard
1 tsp.	Horseradish (optional)
½ cup	Plain breadcrumbs
¾ cup	Flour on sheet of wax paper
¼–½ cup	Puritan oil
•	Low sodium salt and pepper to taste

Mix all ingredients except flour and oil, season patties and chill for one hour. Coat patties in flour, shake off excess, sauté in pan with hot oil until nice and crusty. Place tuna patties on platter and keep warm.

Sauce:

2 8-oz.	Bottles clam juice
1	Lemon, juice only
1½–2 cups	White wine
1	Small jar caviar (red lump fish, 3½ oz.)
¼ cup	Minced spring onions
1 cup	Non-fat sour cream, mixed with 2 tbsp. cornstarch

Pour off excess oil from pan and add clam juice in pan, deglaze pan by scraping all browned pieces. Add lemon juice and onions and bring to boil, reduce by half. Add sour cream with cornstarch, bring to boil, and add wine until you have the right consistency. Sauce should not be pasty. Turn off heat, add caviar, and serve over patties.

Yields: 10–12 Servings

Cal.: 308   *Sod.: 546 mg*   *Fat: 18 g*   *Chol.: 40 mg*

Notes

§

....

....

....

....

....

Don's Citrus Broiled Cornish Hens

4	*Cornish Hens*
½ cup	*Low sodium chicken broth*
1 cup	*Frozen unsweetened raspberries*
¼ cup	*Honey*
1 tbsp.	*Cornstarch*
¼ cup	*Water*

Marinade:

2	*Oranges (juice only, ¼ cup)*
1	*Lime (juice only)*
½ cup	*Olive oil*
½ tsp.	*Tarragon (optional)*
1	*Orange (zest only)*
1	*Lemon (juice only)*
•	*Low sodium salt and pepper to taste*

With a vegetable peeler, peel the skin (zest) of one orange carefully so as to peel only the orange part without the white, which is bitter. Combine the bottom seven ingredients to make your marinade.

With poultry scissors or a sharp knife, cut the back bone out of each hen, first by cutting the right side of the back and then by cutting down the left side of the back and finally remove it. Turn hen over (breast side up) and flatten it out on a hard surface. Marinate the hens for 30–45 minutes. Broil the hens for 10 minutes on each side.

Reduce heat to 375 degrees and bake for an additional 25–30 minutes according to size. Transfer hens onto serving platter and keep warm. Reserve marinade after straining and discarding orange zest. Deglaze broiling pan by scraping all drippings on pan with wire whip after adding marinade. Add chicken broth, raspberries, honey, salt and pepper and boil for about 10 minutes. Mix cornstarch with cold water until dissolved and slowly pour into sauce stirring constantly. Simmer for a few minutes on low heat. To serve, spoon a small bed of sauce on each plate, place hen on top, and sauce on top of hen.

Yields: 4 Servings

Cal.: *700*   ***Sod.:*** *140 mg*   ***Fat:*** *39 g*   ***Chol.:*** *140 mg*

Notes

§

....

....

....

QUAIL ALEXANDRA

½ cup	Uncooked orzo pasta
1 cup	Sliced fresh spinach
8	Boneless Quail
¼ cup	Olive oil
•	Low sodium salt and pepper to taste
•	Sweet paprika

Cook orzo al dente in boiling water with salt. Drain and rinse with cold water. Add sliced spinach and black pepper. Stuff into quails. Rub with oil and sprinkle with salt, pepper and paprika. Bake in preheated oven at 375 degrees for 30–40 minutes. Serve with your favorite sauce.

Yields: 4 Servings

Cal.: 503   *Sod.: 206 mg*   *Fat: 22 g*   *Chol.: 140 mg*

Notes

§

Grilled Salmon Marina

1/3 cup	Orange juice
1/3 cup	Low sodium soy sauce
3 tbsp.	Peanut oil
3 tbsp.	Catsup
1 tbsp.	Honey
1/2 tsp.	Ground ginger
1	Clove garlic, minced
4 4-oz.	Salmon filets

Combine all ingredients except salmon filets. Place salmon in shallow glass dish and top with marinade. Cover and marinate in refrigerator for one hour. Drain salmon, reserve marinade. Grill salmon for five minutes. Carefully turn salmon steaks, brush with reserved marinade and grill five minutes longer or until salmon flakes easily.

Yields: 4 Servings

Cal.: 323   *Sod.:* 1016 mg   *Fat:* 12 g   *Chol.:* 15 mg

Notes

§

ANGEL HAIR PASTA WITH ESCARGOT

4 cans	*Escargot, 12–14 count, drained and washed*
1 lb.	*Angel hair pasta, slightly undercooked*
½ cup	*Minced, fresh parsley for garnish*
½ cup	*Olive oil*
2 tbsp.	*Minced, fresh garlic*
•	*Red pepper flakes for bite*
•	*Low sodium salt and pepper to taste*

Heat oil, add garlic and escargot, sauté briefly. Add all other ingredients, except for the parsley and heat thoroughly. Serve immediately and sprinkle with parsley and extra freshly ground pepper if desired.

Yields: 6 servings

Cal.: 342   **Sod.:** *121 mg*   **Fat:** *10 g*   **Chol.:** *150 mg*

Notes

§

Pork Tenderloin Brent

2 lbs.	Pork tenderloin, sprinkled with low sodium salt and pepper to taste
1/2 cup	Flour
1/4 cup	Olive oil
1 10-oz. jar	Red pepper jelly
1 tspn.	Minced garlic
1/2 cup	White wine
1/2 cup	Low sodium chicken broth or water
2 tbsp.	Corn starch

Coat meat in flour, brown in hot oil, on all sides. Place in pre-heated oven 375 degrees for 25–30 minutes or until done.

Sauce:

Pour jelly in pan with garlic, add wine and boil on low for a few minutes. Mix cornstarch with broth or water and pour into sauce pan. Bring to boil and cook until slightly thickened. Remove from heat. Slice pork into thin, rounded slices and top with sauce.

Yields: 8 Servings

Cal.: *320*   ***Sod.:*** *70 mg*   ***Fat:*** *13 g*   ***Chol.:*** *10 mg*

Notes

§

Pasta Primavera Light

½ lb.	Ziti pasta, cooked al dente
1	Medium green zucchini, cut into 1 inch chunks
1	Medium yellow zucchini cut into 1 inch chunks
1	Yellow pepper cut into strips
1	Medium carrot cut into thin strips
1 head	Broccoli flowerets, stem can be cleaned with vegetable peeler and sliced
1 bunch	Spring onions, cut into 1 inch pieces
2 tbsp.	Fresh basil, cut into strips
1 tbsp.	Fresh minced garlic
1 cup	White wine
12	Small cherry tomatoes for garnish only
1 cup	Freshly grated parmesan
¼ cup	Olive oil
1 cup	Sliced shiitake mushrooms (optional)
•	Low sodium salt and pepper to taste

Sauté vegetables, except cherry tomatoes, with herbs in olive oil with salt, pepper, and garlic for 5–7 minutes. Add pasta, ½ cup cheese and wine. Cook on medium heat until flavors are blended. Taste and adjust spices. Pour in serving dish sprinkle with remaining cheese and garnish with cherry tomatoes.

Yields: 6–8 Servings

Cal.: *338*   ***Sod.:*** *12 mg*   ***Fat:*** *14 g*   ***Chol.:*** *0 mg*

Notes

§

CHICKEN ROMA

1 lb.	Boneless, skinless chicken breasts, trimmed of excess fat
8½ oz.	Can quartered artichoke hearts

Marinade:

½ cup	Olive oil
¼ cup	White vinegar
1 tsp.	Oregano
1 tsp.	Basil
½ tsp.	Minced garlic
•	Red pepper flakes (optional)
•	Low sodium salt and pepper to taste

Mix all ingredients together in a mixing bowl with a whisk. Marinate chicken with artichokes in marinade for 20-30 minutes. Remove chicken and broil for 10 minutes, top with artichokes, and broil 5-10 minutes longer while basting with marinade until golden brown. Great with pesto pasta!

Yields: 4 Servings

Cal.: 366   **Sod.:** 320 mg   **Fat:** 30 g   **Chol.:** 86 mg

Notes

§

JAMAICAN CHICKEN BREAST

1	Small onion
3 tbsp.	Honey
3 tbsp.	Fresh thyme
1 tbsp.	Freshly ground pepper
1 tbsp.	Ground nutmeg
1/2 tsp.	Ground allspice
1/2 tsp.	Red pepper flakes
1/2 tsp.	Low sodium salt
1/2 tsp.	Minced garlic
3 tbsp.	Minced cilantro
1 lb.	Boneless chicken breast, skin and excess fat removed, pounded and cut into four portions

Put all ingredient, except chicken, into blender. Blend into a paste. Pound chicken between two sheets of plastic wrap. Spread paste on both sides of chicken, cover, and marinate for one hour. Broil or grill for five minutes on each side. Serve with mango chutney and rice.

Yields: 4 Servings

Cal.: 271   *Sod.: 144 mg*   *Fat: 5 g*   *Chol.: 87 mg*

Notes

§

OMI'S CRUSHED PINEAPPLE PIE

§

SEAN'S FLOATING ISLAND

§

RASPBERRY FOOL

§

BAKED APPLE IN A JACKET

§

LAURA'S STRAWBERRY DELIGHT

DESSERTS

OMI'S CRUSHED PINEAPPLE PIE

1	Prepared crumb crust of your choice (fat free, 9")
6 oz.	Low fat cream cheese
¼ cup	Sugar
1 20-oz.	Can crushed pineapple, drained
1 lg. tub	Cool Whip

Whip cream cheese with sugar, drain pineapple and fold into cream cheese with spatula. Fold one cup of Cool Whip, into pineapple mixture, until light and airy. Fill into pie shell, and top off with remaining Cool Whip. Chill for 3–4 hours and serve.

Yields: 8 Servings

Cal.: *150* ***Sod.:*** *162 mg* ***Fat:*** *4 g* ***Chol.:*** *11 mg*

Notes

§

Sean's Floating Island

6	*Egg whites (room temperature)*
•	*Low sodium saltb*
¾ cup	*Sugar*
1 capful	*White vinegar*
1 tsp.	*Chambord*
1 tbsp.	*Margarine (to grease casserole dish, 8½" x 8½")*

Preheat oven to 250 degrees. Beat egg whites until foamy. Add salt and vinegar. Add sugar slowly by teaspoons, until stiff and shining peaks are formed. Beat in chambord. Put meringue into greased baking dish and bake for 30–40 minutes in the center of the oven. Cool, loosen sides with knife and unmold onto platter and cover.

Sauce:

1 lb.	*Frozen unsweetened strawberries*
¼ cup	*Chambord*

Blend in blender until smooth. Pour in deep, attractive, large bowl. Cut wedges of meringue and serve floating island on sauce.

Yields: 12 Servings

Cal.: 122   **Sod.:** 19 mg   **Fat:** 1.3 g   **Chol.:** 0 mg

Notes

§

RASPBERRY FOOL

1 pint	Fresh raspberries (optional)
16 oz.	Frozen unsweetened raspberries
1 tbsp.	Cornstarch
¼ cup	Water
16 oz.	Cool Whip
•	Fresh mint for garnish

Defrost raspberries, place in pot and bring to a boil. Mix cold water with cornstarch, stirring out all lumps, and slowly pour into boiling raspberries, stirring occasionally until color turns red again. Chill. Gently fold Cool Whip into mixture. Garnish top of bowl with fresh raspberries and sprigs of fresh mint. Chill and serve.

Yields: 5 Servings

Cal.: *200*   ***Sod.:*** *8 mg*   ***Fat:*** *7 g*   ***Chol.:*** *0 mg*

Notes

§

BAKED APPLE IN A JACKET

1	Sheet puff pastry (store bought)
4	Medium-sized Granny Smith apples, peeled and cored
4 tbsp.	Apricot preserves
½ cup	2% milk for brushing

Fill apples with preserves. Sprinkle work surface with flour and roll out pastry slightly. Cut into four squares and wrap apples completely. Use scraps to cut out little designs for decorating apples. Brush with milk and bake for 45 minutes to one hour, in a preheated 450 degree oven. Don't overcook or apples will lose their shape.

Yields: 4 Servings

Cal.: 130   *Sod.: 45 mg*   *Fat: 1.5 g*   *Chol.: 1 mg*

Notes

§

Laura's Strawberry Delight

4	Large stem glasses
4 cups	Fresh strawberries, remove tops and cut in half, reserve 4 whole for garnish
3 tbsp.	Sugar
2 tbsp.	Balsamic vinegar
8	Amaretto cookies or almond cookies
6 oz.	Cool Whip (Light)

Mix cut strawberries with sugar and balsamic vinegar. Let sit for 45 minutes. Spoon about ¼ cup berries with their juices into each of four glasses. Top each with one cookie and ¼ cup Cool Whip. Repeat berries, cookies, and Cool Whip. Cover and refrigerate at least five hours or overnight. Garnish with whole strawberry on top.

Yields: 4 Servings

Cal.: *231* ***Sod.:*** *50 mg* ***Fat:*** *10 g* ***Chol.:*** *10 mg*

Notes

§

Order Forms

Use the order forms below to obtain additional copies of
Food for your Health.

Fill in order form below, cut out, and mail to:

Helga's Books
3113 Lewis Place
Falls Church, Virginia 22042

Please mail _____ copies of Food for your Health
@ $12.95 each, plus $1.25 shipping and handling per book.
*(Make check payable to **Helga's Books**.)* Mail books to:

Name _____

Address _____

City, State, Zip _____

Telephone (_____) _____

Please print clearly. Allow 2–3 weeks for delivery.

Fill in order form below, cut out, and mail to:

Helga's Books
3113 Lewis Place
Falls Church, Virginia 22042

Please mail _____ copies of Food for your Health
@ $12.95 each, plus $1.25 shipping and handling per book.
*(Make check payable to **Helga's Books**.)* Mail books to:

Name _____

Address _____

City, State, Zip _____

Telephone (_____) _____

Please print clearly. Allow 2–3 weeks for delivery.